Water
and Life

WATER
and
LIFE

Photos, and Poems
In English and Italian

Adolph Caso

BRANDEN BOOKS
Boston

©Copyright 2002
by Adolph Caso

First Edition, 1976

Second Edition, 2002
With photographs and additional poems

Library of Congress Cataloging-in-Publication Data

Caso, Adolph.
    Water and life ; photos, and poems in English and Italian
    / Adolph Caso
    p. cm.
ISBN 0-8283-2079-9 (pbk. : alk. paper)
I. Title.
PS3553.A794 W3 2002
811'.54--dc21

                      2002008310

BRANDEN BOOKS
Division of Branden Publishing Company
P.O. Box 812094 Wellesley MA 02482

To
Margherita

CONTENTS

POEMS IN ENGLISH

POESIE IN ITALIANO

WATER AND LIFE

Flat and round,
infinity
before my eyes:
I see the waves
rolling in,
hitting at my feet--waves
reduced to ripples
of water vanishing
under these feet.
From whence comes life?
Where does it go?
I think of the moon
and see the answer;
and I bend
to scoop a cup
to feel the wonderment
of infinity
trickle down my hands.
Flat and round,
infinity
before my eyes:
I see the waves
rolling in,
hitting at my feet--
soon,
my essence
will come back to you.
I turn around
and see the earth--
valleys deepened
by mountain peaks, like life,
a chain of ups and downs,
desperation and joy.
And I wonder

when, or
why, or
how I
will turn my back
to feel the water
run down these hands
into the essence
from which it came.

THE OCEAN

I've seen mountain tops
though I have spent my life below
as most of us do
on dry and tortuous river beds,
the upper view blocked
by jagged rocks
and steep ravines.

I've been in river floods
taken down by torrents
and felt the nearness
of the ocean's silent mouth.

If I owe this life to anything
it was
as it will be
to sprawling trees
bent in sacrifice
or the rock
that lifts up
from the fatal current.

I see myself
in drops of water
that spill before my feet
from the splash beneath
and slowly disappear
in drying.

To these
I compare my life--
my eyes shrunk and dry
to behold the mountain top
growing in height.

LEAVES IN ADORNMENT

The wind has finally ceased;
a breeze of drizzly rain
accompanies the leaves to the ground
while trees tower above
                beds
of multi-colored leaves
in last adornment.
Tree trunks stand as tombs,
their branches
                tentacles against the sky
beneath which the colors
unknowingly disappear.

Drops linger and roll off
absorbed by the ground--
a handkerchief moist with tears
speechless and dispassionate
while above
the camouflage
undergoes
one more eternal change.

WHITE CLIFFS

The speaker's voice
a solo
above the crowd's whispering--
nonsense
at different levels
both, or all
telling
what has and needs be done,
while below
at the edge of the cliff
the water keeps on rolling in,
forming waves
               older
than human consciousness.

The speaker's voice
a solo
above the whispers.

The sea gulls fly by the window
dipping through the air
scanning waves
that bear the fruit;
and I wonder
whether it be better
to be a man
               capable
of seeking food
and still be starved
or
the sea gull scanning the waves
and catch its fish.

FOUNT CLITUMNUS

The single swan
proudly breaks
the lustral waters
of Fount Clitumnus
down
at the foot of the mountain
surrounded by tall poplars
whose leaves patter
to the light breeze
of a June meridian wind,
the quietness in the air
broken
by the hum of a distant car
by the trout
sprung to surface
quickly disappearing
amidst the multiplying ripples
that slowly fade
into infinity.

The blue sky
reflecting
to the bottom of the pool
dancing
with the suspended weeds
along the edge:
nymphs from ancient Rome
moving to the rhythm
of woodwind sounds
scanning the trees,
the leaves pattering
to a definite beat,
their shimmering green
reflected down deep

        to the floating weeds
all
ritually dancing
        in my imagination.
Nature
transfigured
the mind inebriated of wine
the sight
lingering over breasts of nymphs
dancing

in the transparent waters
for ages
        un-thirsting
to animal and man
under the cool shadows
of the poplars
in which Silenus,
with his magic reeds,
hides his bearded face
while the single swan
        mindless
of life or death
eats and drinks
as though
neither
        I nor Silenus
have
or
will ever be.

QUI TOLLIS PECCATA MUNDI

"QUI TOLLIS PECCATA MUNDI..."
The car radio
emitting voices in chorus
of a high mass
beneath towering oaks and maples
whose leaves in full colors
drop aimlessly
onto a moist ground
of soft expansive beds
of red and golden hues,
amidst water drops,
flickering
from beams of light
in a multitude of trajectories
through leaves and branches
dancing above the shimmering
beds of leaves,
and,
"Qui tollis peccata mundi..."
voiced by male and female voices--
a chorus coming together as one
building to rhythmic crescendos
like waves at sea on calm days.

My body,
still within its silent rapture,
my soul,
full of sights and sounds--
instants comprised
in units of ecstacy and happiness
in full communion,
and, sinless:

"Qui tollis peccata mundi..."

A POET'S END

Alone,
he seeks the sky of night
the dark of day
the winding road
of death's
sinuous paths
in and between
hills of phantasms.

What makes him drive?
What makes him return?
What mental haunts
take from one end
and give the other
unconsummated passions?
What seeks to destroy his soul?
Who wants to take his body away?

Deep sky
and core of earth:
Why
do you abound
within this miserable bit of man
who tries to bring together
into a moment
pre-destined poles
and God?

In his last moment,
what makes him look?

The peace
forever fleeting like spoken words
or
the realization of death
once the harbinger of peace
that does not exist?

God!
stretch your hand
a little further.

DON QUIXOTE

Loren lips
haunt
every cell of my body--
eyes
translucent in mine
like images
passing through prisms
each a spear for a different torment
the stimulus of lust
awakened
to arrows that drive deeper
into the live flesh
in hunger

and you
are not here
to assuage the pain!

I'm like the starfish
hovering beds
of numberless shells
awaiting a current
to put them in tide
while all around
life throbs
            indifferent
to its hunger.

When I find you
will I kiss your lips
and be myself again
or those of Dulcinea
and run the plains
            in search
of what will not be there
and fight
            the dragons
                        in my mind?

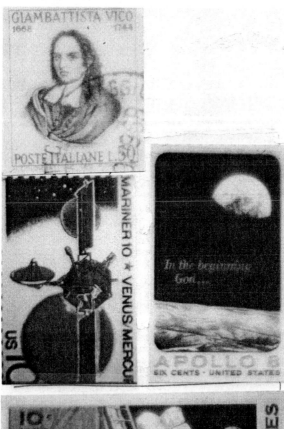

GIAMBATTISTA VICO
1668   1744

POSTE ITALIANE L. 30

MARINER 10 ★ VENUS/MERCURY

US 10c

In the beginning
God...

APOLLO 8
SIX CENTS · UNITED STATES

10c
AIR MAIL

FIRST MAN ON THE MOON   UNITED STATES

VICHIAN CYCLES

The cold count-down
followed
by the blast-off
that sends you
                into space
through
          oxymoronic layers
that bend in the heavens
for an instant
and quickly close
as though
                man
had never been present.

Your processed voice
comes to me
as you speed through space
toward the moon,
your mind intent
              on instruments
my heart
              pounding
as you draw away from me.

Will you ever come back!

Though you know
the point of your arrival
I wonder
              in dread excitement
over your feat of maneuverability
and intelligence;
when I hear your voice
the space becomes vast.
My feet

on the ground
I get dizzy thinking
you may reach
a point of no return--
the concomitant
            lost and found--
and myself
            neither
                and
                    without
the guidance you're receiving.

Even after the moon registers
your footprint
                and our cloth,
I shudder over your return
through layers of chaos
like fingers
                plucking
the harpsichord
the sound from the first string
lasting
or
sustained by another
to make a whole possible--
noise to harmony
order to chaos!

Vichian cycles
of spiraling circles
will bring you back
            to me
purer
for having passed
        through layers
                of
                    purifying fire.

LOVE POEM

I have loved you
with all my heart and soul
more
          than you could ever imagine,
the prime time
when your breast was full,
its touch
the wondrous excitement
and the deep thrust
into your fertile womb
of joy and life,
the wonderment of my being
into yours,
completely yours
heart and soul,
the mystery of love
unfolding
with every touch,
every thought--
acts reduced to words of love
full of meaning--
complete life
received into your body
like the tremors
of Dante's quake
and the birth of one more soul.

That was the joy I felt
as on a continuum,
without beginning or end--
all this in the words of love
I whispered into your ears,
kissed on your lips,
into your mouth--
within the receptive womb
bathed by life's semen
caressed by the palm of your hand
in excitement

for the gift of life's process
tingling
within every part of your body;

And all was love,
and in how many ways I said it,
showed it,
bathed you with the pure water of life,
my life
        vigorous
            vibrating
wondrous growth
                  fulfillment
of untold life's mysteries
permeating the semen
implanted in the womb
to fertilize and grow,
the potential of life
uncovered through you,
the total
            reduced
to the word of love,
the pure water of life
with which I bathed you,
and the excitement was yours
more than you could ever imagine
though you brought your hand down
to caress the receptive womb
in which life
        was already
            germinating,
and you were happy,
        ecstatic
serenely exuberant,
and my words of love to you
reverberated through my body--
the sounds and glances
          a seance
to your ears and eyes:
        magic
quietly dancing

in sparkles reflected
over the rolling waves
of the soft sea at sunrise
after the explosion of a storm.

All this still within me
completely imprisoned
hermetically sealed
with layers upon layers
like rings in a tree-trunk
solidly encasing
impermeable to cracks
not to expose
               the inner core
of suffering!

What layers can the heart take
when the mind knows none
the passions feel no bounds
and the pressure builds!

Will the moment come
when love will explode
like a volcano at sea:
will it be an island
thrusting out
with its words of smoke
and absorbed into the newly-born land
or
        one
             disappearing
                   beneath the sea
with its words of smoke
                  wasted
to the wind?

I have loved you
with all my heart and soul,
more than you can ever imagine,
and still do
though that prime of life

will not return.
And vain it is,
for time is never lost
like life
on a continuous bend
every moment a new discovery
progression within control
always going forward
and never back.

Oh that I should not be able to go back
into
        those journeys,
                in vain,
for nothing goes back,
not even the island or non-island at sea,
not even the surface of the ocean
or that of the land
or the layers of the air
that form the skies.
We can catapult
with or without conscience,
and like the island or non-island at sea
we will come back,
the words of love like the smoke
absorbed by the land
                        or
wasted to the wind.

I have loved you
with all my heart and soul.

And this return of no return
is like powder forced into a chamber
the explosion
to reveal
the inner core
the beginning of another beginning
the end of another end
and never
the beginning or the end.

Like the volcano at sea,
will it give an island
or take one;
like our words,
the smoke absorbed
or
wasted to the wind?

Love is not a word
not a fantasy.
It is there--
                    here!
in my heart
awake or dormant
much as it is in you--
prime life forever when awake
smoke wasted to the wind
when dormant;
the volcano ready to erupt
and build toward the sky
or disappear
into the core of the earth.

I want to love you
more than you can ever imagine
And when I do
and you are there
the words of love will explode
like volcanos at sea
thrusting islands
into
            the
                skies.

EVENING OF SPRING

A fresh wind rolled down the hill
bringing a new force of life
to the quivering grass
amidst which
she and I walked.
What splendor of night!

The moon made its way across the sky
while webs of tiny branches
whispered in unison:
Here they are; here they are,
the God-made couple.
I brought my hand to her breast
and there beheld paradise.

MOUNTAIN DUSK

Flakes
that fall infinite
to human sight,
extensive horizons
that melt with the sun--
soft and smooth is the earth;
its branches
                quiver
                        to the wind.
Dusk!
        the change that few see:
whirls
of silvery granules
                    roll along
and disappear in ballads
that go on
so long
the flicker of light remains
on the dying day
and sparks
                refract
from the icy snow.

TANGLEWOOD

How could I not stare
at the violin section
whose music
ran through my spine.
My lips trembled
for want of taste
and my eyes closed.

"What is it you feel?"
She asked,
this woman next to me.

"That it should touch your heart,"
I answered in a glimpse
and closed my eyes
to lock within
the memory of a moment
about to disappear.

RUTH

I see spring in your eyes--
vast areas of green
sprouts
swaggering offsprings
with touches of dew.

Then summer ablaze
and the harvest reaped.

With autumn,
the entwining
and the sweet melancholy--
moments of warmth
change
into tepid feelings
of a sun setting.

Then winter comes to your eyes,
and how clear this winter is
though your eyes are green.

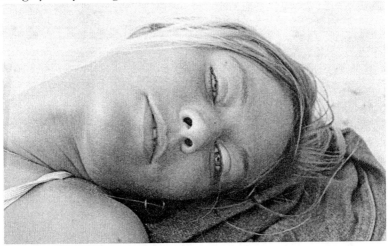

TWO TRINKETS

What to make of the head
semi-glued to its cracking pedestal:
both seem to contain
and be driven
by a force not yet revealable
or understandable--
yet brittle as the matter containing the earth
and malleable as that containing the brain.

Touch the first with any tool;
drop it on the ground,
or bang it in any way,
and you will have accomplished permanence.

Repeat the process
(willing or not),
and you will have completed
another permanence.

Look at the pedestal--
once flat, and transparent of earth,
now wobbly and brittle,
ready to break into pieces
by the earth's forces
emanating from within,
pushing and pulling
to gain a freedom
in another counter force.

What can we make of it all?
What can you make of the face
now reflecting yours truly?

Apply the forces of your will,
squeeze it between your fingers,

or let an accident get to it,
and you will have changed
its life form forever,
and another taken its place.

As both come to you,
well wrapped in soft tissue
covered by yet another layer of paper--
receipt in hand,
I entrusted them
to the laws of another conduit.
How will they reach you?
More importantly,
What will reach you?

Someday, that it should never come!
out of anger or negligence
you can always refer
to the defects of the conduit
with its multifarious secret laws.

Amidst these things
and considerations,
reflecting on the continuous changes
of us and in us all,
that which remains eternal
is that which takes place
and preserved in our minds.

If it pulses with blood
flowing through our hearts,
it is love
and not subject to counter forces
or to conduits
beyond the reach of our hand.

How they will reach you,
or, what will reach you
does not matter;
they are under the control
and the energy of someone else,
and made of clay.

Unlike our love of yesteryear,
will the earth remain in one piece
like the statue of yours truly?
Or will their conduit
be given to accounting
tomorrow's earth
broken into pieces
and tomorrow's statue
turned into another amorphous form?
Does so much
need to be a life of trinkets!

LIPPI'S MADONNA

My testicles
gently pressed
against your buttocks,
my arm
extended over your side,
my hand
cuffing your soothing breast,
my head
floating on the feathery pillow
as my eyes open and close:
the conscious
blissfully
surrendering to the unconscious.

And,
in the morning's early light,
your face
assumes the soft glow
of Fra Lippo Lippi's
madonna on the throne.

AN EVENING

How calm is the sea
                smooth
with hardly a ripple
to break its lustrous surface.
Listen,
there is a hush in the air.

The moon slowly creeps
from behind the hills
casting a kiss across the bay
while my soul engulfs the water
and shatters itself
amidst
        the myriad tiny ripples
that sparkle beneath the ray--
there's magic in the air.

My ears follow the silence;
the eyes pursue the stars;
my body lifts and soars
behind a moment of eternity--

Drink of it, hungry you are
like a new-born child
                suckling
closes his eyes.

I CALL YOU GOD

I've fixed you in a statue
and called you God--
your attributes
not those of stone
over which
I've worked
to capture
              a moment
of fleeting immortality.
Have I?
The hardest rock
crumbles with time.
I look at yesterday's flower,
at your face,
all resolving
into un-recallable moments
that live and follow us
through every step
every passion
and keenest desires--
changing
always and forever changing.

I've fixed you in a statue
and called you
God.

SILENT, THE ROCKS

Cool and silent is the peak
covered by lifeless shadows
and the color of the moon's
pale streaks.
Un-designated trees enjoy
a rampant breeze
while rows of rocks
speak their sorrows.

Do not be dazed; say the rosary.
This rock is not the stone
over which you wept before.
The sun has never shone here.

Rows of rocks weep over the sorrows
the anguishes that rooted them down.
Who knows of the bones in the burrows
or the steel that once
                   was the crown
of men forgotten.
The symbol hangs on
though the rocks remain
over which to weep.

Come, old woman in black,
assemble the twigs of the deep.
Do not stop.
The stone is not your son's.
Below, your children await the fire.
Go!
Nourish them!
Another peak awaits.

"WHAT DID I DO?"

I thought of you,
daughter of woman,
while walking along
the Mohawk Trail
ablaze
      burning
the multi-colored leaves
ephemeral
as this I nurture.

I saw the air
prepare the trees for winter,
and here and there
a branch
      already wept
              above
its reddened earth.

THE OLD MAN

Alone
      he sits
on the solitary hillside
silently looking at the ground
the hands on the shiny cane
the hat
on the heap of dirt
his eyes
      piercing and aflame
the mind thinking
          about eternity
in a world
        eternally around:

"I am of you,
not you of me,"
he said
silently
to himself
as he sat
on that solitary hillside
powerless
of what was coming
and satisfied
to rest his hat
on the heap of dirt--
God
had not yet shown
his face.
How many lifetimes had passed
and
      HE
not shown His face?
The old man pondered.

How many more will pass
before
a single glance,
            a clue,
to whatever!

On the solitary hillside
the old man sits
            alone
in a world eternally around
and he,
powerless,
solitary,
poised,
looks at the sun
brilliantly setting
over the other hill--
how many times before,
how many more
will he have
        to uncover his head
and place the hat
on the heap of dirt
even if tomorrow
Eternity should come?

SENSITIVITY

Slowly,
his foot goes forward
his head bending
                    with each step
taken
through the silent road.

The crisp leaves crackle
under the feet
                    that deal
the unexpected blow.

Come,
return to your room;
enclose all that's within you,
and lie on your bed
like the paralyzed leaves
awaiting the unsolicited wind
that will put
                    their quivering
membranes
        to flight.

FLY BIRD!

Fly, fly,
                fly away
from the hunter
that pursues you.

Dip, rise,
swerve and dive.
Deceive
        the hunter's sight.

If the fire takes you,
drop!

If life is still within,
hide
        into a hole
of the earth
and bask
        with the snake.

DOLORE

His mouth,
semi-wide and tense,
opened and closed
with each blow
of the hammer
that pierced
his hands
to the cross.

What pain, or sorrow,
was felt,
his eyes
did not show
though wrinkles
surrounding the cavities
expanded
and drew tight
with each blow.

NOVEMBER 22, 1963

A shot rings

in my ears;

its bullet

pierces

my heart.

Tears,

     shed!

GOD ! WHEN WILL IT BE

Here you are
unrecognizable.
It seems you've just come out
of an old newspaper wrap
tossed in a corner
to be forgotten.

Who helped?
Who discovered you?
What unseen hand
                    lifted away
the stifling veil?

The miracle has taken place
though not quite as Lazarus,
or
was it Lazarus that lived
or
just his name!

You're still unrecognizable
though the print is clear.
You look for the strongest links,
and when you find them
the secret still be missing.
God,
            when will it be!

WHY DREAM?

Why dream, he said,
that haggard man of wisdom;
live not with your dreams.
Unfulfilled passions are rivers
lost in vapors.
Go, dig:
the things you do
are those which make you.
Don't live
as a part of someone
bigger
       than you.
Create or destroy:
envy is born with age,
the stage that you will reach
without the breach
of cause and effect.
Why worry?
Life is very bold we are told
by sages reaching their end.
They spend their days in thoughts.
Run:
fulfill those urges
that surge within your soul.

Kiss:
if you don't do it now
you will miss the bliss
that attracts the young.
And if you can,
follow the cycles
as winter follows autumn.
The break is never present
to prevent the fulfillment

you desire.
We shall all taste the ocean,
deep with grief and wide with hope
No one can cope with the ocean,
the god of rivers
                    which bend
as do our lives.
We meander to hold back time,
the prime offender of our lives.

MY KISSES LIVED AS THE ROSE

My kisses lived as the rose!
In those ecstatic moments I felt
sweet caresses of the wind
and the vigor
of a thousand sparkling drops of dew.
Green diffused in vermillion,
and red dazzled the image within the eye;
Dark were they of olive deep purple
that entranced each kiss. Deeper
still were the velvet twinings
wrapping their arms around the branches
and losing themselves in the suave twining
of purple hue. The quivering grass
from beneath secrete the ascending
perfume of vigor, and the descending
light bathes them with toxic excitement.
the sibilant winds go singing through embraces
with notes of the exotic and the erotic.
The rain excites the roots to the movements
and the streaks of lightening glitter,
thrusting its baton into sensuality.

And all then moves in awesome rhythm.

Trickling water ripples itself away.
Within the limpid air, the rays of the sun mix
and the spiritual atmosphere becomes king.
Smiles and sweet kisses get lost in shades.
Time passes; the water ripples itself away,
and those kisses live as my Rose.

THE JOURNEY

Dress up:
match the trousers to the jacket
not forgetting the sox.
Pass the tie around the collar,
balance the incision below the knot,
and shine the diamond with the cloth.

Brush your hair with the comb
your mother gave you
when it was thin and silky--
with loving care she'd part it.

Focus your face in the mirror
you bought as old. No!
Don't rub your face;
the fuzziness's on the glass.

Hurry, it's getting late.
The class will soon begin.
Don't bother to ask your mother
how you look, for, she is old
and illiterate. She thinks only
of making ends meet, and reflects
on good and evil.
At times, when she reveals her soul to you,
you look on with mindful patience.

Those wrinkles on her face
did not come as a result of age
but she could bridge the gap
with special paste, you say.
And you are right.
Hurry. You must go to class.
The professor is ready
to talk about the poet's journey
to Hell, Purgatory and Paradise.

COMPETITION

I want to surround my house
with lawns softer than carpets
for people to tread upon
or smear
or step upon at will.
I'm intent on making it
free of crab-grass
and of other
undesirable elements
that should make it
short of perfect.
I will cut down trees
of any age
ugly or pretty
which might take the sprinkled water
from its roots.
I'll supervise the growth
and check its daily advancement
weeding out,
                as is done,
in the process of our very lives.

And I shall die weeding grass
and cutting trees.

When the moment comes,
not remember the harm
or know what I have done,
except to wonder
                     when
I shall weed
            or be myself
weeded out.

IDLENESS

Poet,
what are thou?
A man
of yesteryear,
today,
and tomorrow,
of your heart
speaker
      of waveless seas
and windless air
which we see not
or touch
and yet despair?

VERSES?

I dare not cry
for fear
the tears
will drool
all over the verses.
"What verses!"
I have read Virgil and Dante,
Petrarch and Leopardi.
Nevertheless,
I ask
        because
I know the necessity of evil--
the constant battle
that makes our lives possible.
And so
I go on expressing thoughts
whatever the form or trend.

Evil is still the same:
unchangeable and true,
in free association with some,
the perennial conscience of many-
I allow myself to think.
But never a moment of this
has lolled me into sleep.

CAPITAL PUNISHMENT

Capital punishment!
the carry-over
of past social savagery
into our modern
civilized
       society.
"I will not have
any part of it,"
says
       the shopkeeper
while surrounding
himself
       with
G U N S F O R S A L E

"If you believe
and want them,
I will keep an open mind
so long you're
           twenty-one"

ON MY WAY

Never the desire has left me
to get to you, oh God,
in these last thirty years
and some, of which so many
in darkness.
Are there more?

I should not ask the question
for night is yet my light
that fluctuates so distantly
though close to my heart:
too often,
it dimly disappears.

So with the means--religion,
with all the man-made sinuousness
whose beauty and logic
have often brought me close to you.
You,
        remained distant
                and dim.

Still,
I lay in thought of you
not knowing how much of it,
or the inner being,
is my feeling.

FAME ASSURED

Our heads turn to each other
awaiting the speaker
to come
to enlighten us.
Our chatter mixes
with the smoke
that slowly rises
to the silent ceiling
that absorbs everything.
Whatever is lost
no doubt is small
in spite of the years
of accumulation,
one would think
should dull at least
the color of the paint.
Nothing is lost:
no sounds, no images
go beyond
the retaining ceiling
whose lights shine like stars
we often take as real.
The whispers stop
as the speaker takes the step
onto the podium.
The joke.
The laughter.
The wheels of the recorder
spin
       indifferent
to the voice or laughter.
Thus,
our desires for glory and fame
are assured,
and
     great
          becomes
what was once the common thing.

NEW YEAR'S EVE

Midnight
has struck an instant
un-recordable.
Past and future
        meet
like the tinkle of two,
three glasses of champagne
about to disappear
before smiling lips
and eager eyes.
Embraces
caresses
kisses
assuage the pain
that disappears
into resolutions
of short-lived moments of joy.

Shouts
        cries
desperation
           tears
resound uncontrolled
beneath the lights
that flicker
through the eternal prism.

An instant
        un-recordable
creates
      the jungle
of inception and of death--
rivers of emotions overflowing
all
ending and beginning

at one time.
New Year's Eve:
a tinkling of glasses,
a kiss prolonged,
one lifetime,
the moment
          that was
and never will be.

THE BRICK JUNGLE

Bricks
interposed by iron and stone,
the moonlight
held back from corners
where shadows breathe
with human hearts,
the empty spaces
crossed by palpitating kisses
of sharp arrows
and dark lines of escape:
these spread above the brick jungle
of countless human spirits that live,
traversed by shades of light,
in the depth of which a baby's voice
cries out
        confounded
in the cruel cradle
of solitude and bars.

Out on the resounding sidewalks
children run and play
unaware of the web of lines
pricked by sounds of tears.
Oblivious are the lips that kiss
in the winding corridors crossed
by brick doorways of spears.
A lonely saxophone sings its blues
to the voluptuous bodies of bare humans,
lost within the boundaries of lines
and the architecture of fire escapes
on the ground.

Further,
a mass of flesh moves about
in the flickering lights of the arcade,
a jungle made alive
                    by screams of women
who've seen themselves transformed
by the warping mirrors
that post the sign:
YOU'VE SEEN REALITY.

JAZZ CHIMERA

Beat the drum to start the tempo;
strike the cymbals
for a silvery tone;
sound the sax
for an indigo mood;
let the horn
sing out in despair.

Sing all
with disconcerted sounds.

Combine the pastoral
to the storm
with clarinets and strings,
the thunder with the base
and the fury of a gong.

Let the bodies quiver from within
and build
the jazz's chimerical beat
into a tantrum
of ecstatic expectation.

YOUTH

"Nineteen years old," she said
as the fresh wind came rolling down
from top of the hill. I blushed.
I was older.
The thought of robbing the cradle
seized me:
"I wish I were young," I said,
more to myself selfishly.
"I wish I were younger," I repeated
not knowing yet
                        how young
I really was.
                        Younger,
I dare say.
Never
            have I traveled the four corners
of the world
                        or seen
the skin roll up my arm
like a parched diploma.

Time,
I hate you.

The wind that soothes the skin
is never the same.

We grow and ask ourselves
how much we've grown--
two, three folds:
is rather slow for this age.

I will see
                        the four corners of the world,

and it's doomed I should.
"I will too, one day," I answered.
She understood and sighed.
Time!
You've hurried those lips to smile,
the eyes to glisten,
the breast to fill;
that mystic harmony,
a trace of sensuality. No!
I do not want to travel
the corners of the world.

BURSTING BALLOONS

When an idea comes to me
to be accomplished in the future
I speak of it in the present
as though it already is
accepted and praised.

And this is the beginning
of the glory
of self-inflated moments
and of daydreams unfulfilled.

Though I quite realize it,
I give in to dreaming:
I fabricate the best of castles,
invent string-held bombs in air
as mines against the planes,
and visualize
                  the world
into one nation.

But when I go beyond,
an itch or noise
brings me back
as a weak point or pin
in a floating balloon.

THE NEW GURU

In guru garb
she sits on the sidewalk,
her face
toward the sun,
the hands binoculars
around the eyes
aimed in full direction
of the fire,
contemplating
the blinding light
of high noon.

The traffic going by
the children on the ground
the music from the doors
like shadows
from puppets
of Socrates' men
chained to the walls
of his cavern.

Women
sunken to the bone
the thin protruded breast
elastic
into emaciated children's mouths-
all
       dying
              of starvation:
decrepits!
      derelicts
             carcasses strewn about
enlivened by scattered cries
of mourning doves

or screeches
            of children
not yet learnt to slowly die
in silence.
            India!
to the Guru
like the blinder to a horse,
binoculars around the eyes
to better hold
the phantasms in eyeballs
that can no longer see.

A HIPPIE'S PROTEST

From a life, rich
of every want
never felt the pangs of hunger
or the feet touch the ground
other than the cool grass
on lawns made beautiful
by some Puerto Rican
working for some Italian
or on wall-to-wall carpets
shampooed as necessary
to keep the shag from knotting
beneath the feet,
the color television
screening images
of peroxide blonds on martinis,
the gratuitous killings,
words of lasting peace
amidst reports of battle slaughters,
the Watergate--from the small
to the big un-necessity
perpetrated by preacher politicians
scoring the recipients
of welfare checks
the crying babies with their emaciated faces,
farmers clad in *genovese* cloth
patched wherever their skins and bones
have worked through
to the harsh bruises of labor,
and the affluent youth
protesting it all--
a rebel through lengthened hair,
barefoot on warm days,
the wheels of a supercharged beetle,
sixteen-speed bikes,

the girl wearing tailored jeans
shed at the feet,
discolored as though
sweat had perspired through,
patched with embroidered monograms
wearing America's flag
the stars on one
the stripes over the other cheek
and the mast wiggling its way up her ass,
wishing it were real!

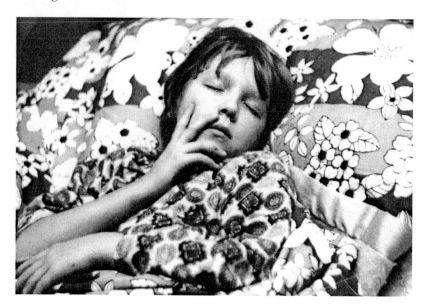

THE NEW ADAM AND EVE

The puffed-up male
noisily following the partner
into the spring foliage
of the tree,
the branches sprawling
over the gurgling waters
of the cool brook
bending
around the foot of the mountain,
where ponds of still waters
are visited
by hovering flies
which quickly disappear;
the tadpoles
the trout
white butterflies
aimlessly
peaking and dipping through the air
the eagle from up on high
the animals wandering
through the virgin land
the bee
winging itself from flower to flower
the honey drops
exuding
from fruits ripened by the sun
the mountain lion
the rattler
raccoons in hide--
the limpid sunset:
all
an impressive spectacle
a dream come true
for the young run-a-way couple,

the new franciscans
wearing the single robe and cord
drinking the waters from the spring
putting together the abandoned cabin
with trees
cut with their own hands
finally free
independent
living the youthful days
in vigorous bodies
singing to birds and animals alike:
Adam and Eve
cast-off
of their city and God,
away from the massive followers of Krishna
from the new materialism
finally free and independent
in their newly gained paradise
there at the foot of the mountain
near the river bed
free from beer cans and bottles
under the watchful eye of the eagle
satisfying today's hunger
with present finds
to run the risk
of being another's meal
than to be consumed piece-meal
through corroborated programs
free of newspaper print
strewn all over the land
or
piles to be processed
without leaving a single trace
of its real mafia
free at last
to wander about nature's spectacle
with hair ruffled by the breeze

bodies of healthy muscles
from years of meat diet and sports
eating nature's food
without the sacrificial offerings
of slaughtered pigs and cows
finally free and independent
enjoying the time of day
in and out
of the wooden shack--
the new Eve, in the presence of Adam,
taking today's pill
     so
          that
               they
can
     get
          laid.

SUICIDE THROUGH MURDER

Blood
I will give
as water
enough to invigorate a boxer
for another round:
Suicide
      through
          murder!

One hundred victims--
five times one hundred
pints of blood
lost to the ground
unredeemably wasted.

Collect for the doomed
what is left of the doomed
having still one breath
of blood
in its warm flesh,
the transfusion
to rehabilitate
for another battle--the spectacle
to keep
our peace-loving hearts
secretly
entertained:
Suicide
      through
          murder!

Blood of yellow today
brown tomorrow
black and white--the secret hope

to quench the ultimate thirst.
It is well
the ground to soak today
tomorrow another ground
and you will give me enough--
just enough--
for another battle--
to your heart's content
secretly
the PEACE button
on your breast:
Suicide
      through
           murder!

Suicide:
cowardice or courage
the latter lacking
allow the victim
to take the blood
of another victim
and you don't want me
to be
the victim of the victim
so long others
are currently available
though enough of yours
you will save for me
and others to follow--
always others!
Suicide
      through
           murder!

For me!
my brothers!
my children!

and theirs!
Five pints of blood
times one thousand
redeemable
transfusable
five times one million
PEACE on heart
blue turned red:
frenetic excitement--
Peace!
      Peace!
            so long
the ground soaks.

If there be peace
you know
you will die:
Suicide
      through
           murder!

POESIE
IN
ITALIANO

ENTRERÒ

Buia è la caverna
ed ho paura di entrarvi.
Vieni con me;
fammi coraggio:
assicurarci la vita
e godere
insieme
il miracolo
d'un'altra scoperta.

TROVARMI IN TE

Sono in cerca di me stesso
e non so
se mi troverò.
Ho il cuore e la mente;
se voglio, posso
trovare
te e me stesso--
comunicarci
se anche tu
con il cuore e la mente
mi cerchi:
non trovarci
sull'onda tarata
di droghe;
il bacio
l'abbraccio
il darci la mano.

Dobbiamo ancora
scoprire noi stessi,
me stesso!
Il morso di vipera uccide;
non chiedermi
d'ingerire il veleno
per l'esperienza.

Trovare me stesso
in te!

RICORDANZE

Qui il posto natale
ove vidi i primi prati verdi,
campi dorati di frumento,
valli sperse ai monti,
ruscelli fluenti;
qui il posto dei primi respiri
dove sentii l'aria
accarezzar il viso
e i raggi del sole
rispecchiar negli occhi.

Qui son tornato
a raggiungere l'amor.

AECLANUM

Più le giornate assolate
che di vento
prorompono
sulla vetusta Aeclanum
morta
da tante generazioni,
dimenticata,
sebbene il genere umano
si tramandi e viva
sulle rovine
di pietre e di ossa umane
sparse
fra le casupole nei dintorni
ove il fico e il ciliegio,
abbandonati
presso lo squarcio archeologico,
offrono la loro frutta purpurea
ai silenziosi spiriti sotterranei--
induriti anche loro
come le zolle di terra
impietrite dal sole
che curva la schiena
dei pochi derelitti
intenti a porre il seme
lí
dove tutto è asciutto e duro,
nel pieno silenzio del giorno
quando si ode la punta dell'aratro
rompere la terra,
lo schiocco della frusta
sulle ossa dure del bove,
il borbottio dell'uomo striminzito
che saltella da una zolla all'altra
come un passero--

la sua donna dietro,
vestita di panni scuri,
con fazzoletto dorato in testa:
viso taciturno
di una donna medioevale
in un trittico bizantino.

LO *STOCCHIO*

Dammi lo stocchio
che io beva
dalla botte
quel vino puro
della mia campagna,
e ubriacarmi
tanto
da gettarmi
sdraiato
a braccia aperte
guardando
il sole
che fa crescere
il quadrifoglio fresco
intorno al mio corpo.

Dammi lo stocchio
che io ribeva!

LA *COMETA*

Non più l'ingannevole vento
porterà via l'aquilone
pazientemente incollato
con la resina del solo ciliegio
che guarda la vetusta Aeclanum.

La sicura mano controlla
il filo di lana disfatto
dall'ultima calza
che la mamma
aveva conservato per l'inverno.

Pian piano scorre il filo
tra le dita che lo trattengono
per un attimo contro il vento
che strappa un istante all'eterno.
La mano guida l'aquilone
che ondeggia sicuro
sopra gli occhi attenti
un po' socchiusi di gioia:

Vento, cielo, Aeclanum
tra le punta delle dita
e il sorriso ingenuo del bimbo.

NAPULE BELLA MIA

Ti ricordo, Napule bella mia,
quando fanciullo ti lasciai
pieno d'entusiasmo e commozione
accompagnato
d'un'armonia di confusione.

Ti ricordai, Napule bella mia,
quando viaggiai per altre terre
ovunque trovando un ordine
e tutto entro quest'ordine.

E tu,
       non c'eri:
non c'era quel fiore che incita l'occhio
all'abbraccio irresistibile.

Napule bella mia,
di te tutto è bello e affascinante.
Tutto vive; tutto è vita
anche nella *zona del silenzio*
dove i motori si sentono a tutta rabbia
e le trombe rimbombano di prepotenza:
"Levateve 'a nanze, aggia passà io!"

Sei tutta vita, Napule bella mia,
che si specchia negli occhi
dei tuoi figli eredi esaltanti:

"Songh'e Napule!"
Napule bella mia.

NAPULE, NAPULE

Napule, Napule:
sole, mare, ammore,
mo,
me miett'a cantà.

Ammore mio
da quanno
te ne sì ghiuta
io non canto
non canto cchiù
cchiù io non canto.

Napule, Napule,
addò staie?
Pecchè a voce toia
non a sento cchiù,
e a museca
addò stà?

Ammore mio
da quanno
te ne si ghiuta
io non ammo
non ammo cchiù
cchiù io non ammo.

Napule, Napule
addò staie?
L'ammore d'aiere
'un ce stà cchiù...
quanto tiempo ancora
adda passà?

Napule, Napule:

sole, mare, ammore
mo me mett'à cantà
Napule, Napule
a musica nun ce stà!

Aint'o suonno
m'a nnata
na criatura
bella cchiù do sole
de no iurno 'e maggio,
cchiù cuieta e allumenosa
de na luna 'e luglio.
E mmo,
come me pozzo tenè
aint'all'anema
sta voce sfrenata:

Napule, Napule:
sole, mare, ammore
me miett'a cantà;
a museca 'n ce stà.
Quanno te spoglio
co chist'uoccie scure,
tu m'aregne ste mmane
de n'acqua fresca e ddoce;
e quann 'a voce toia
m'accarezza sti recchie
te sent'int'a sto core
e canta e canta
a nun fernì,
Napule, Napule:
sole, mare, ammore...

SANDRA BICCE

Lí, attaccata all casa
c'è la camera
di Sandra Bicce,
giovane Americana
che parla italiano
anche al suo gatto
siamese.

È qui per imparare
i costumi del paese;
e per questo, spesso,
va a mangiare
(alle due di notte)
pomodori ripieni di riso
e spaghetti
alla matriciana
dalla Cantina
piena di giovani stranieri
come lei.

Il povero gatto,
lasciato a casa,
passa la notte miagolando
o parlando con altri gattoni
che si fermano alla porta
uno dopo l'altro
come ombre
notturne.

Quel gatto siamese
l'ha portato dall'America
e lo tiene isolato,
chè, nessuno,
o per scherzo o altre ragioni,

apra la porta
e lasciarlo libero.

(Ma, come si può
in Italia
tener sempre la porta chiusa)?

Accadde una sera,
(alle tre di mattina)
un giovanotto italiano,
amico, visto Sandra
accumular un po troppi affetti
al felino, subito capì
che fare.

Ad un tratto
l'animale, spiando
la porta semi aperta,
saltò giù
e subito se la fece
per la porta semi chiusa
con la costernazione di Sandra,
che piangeva.

Di mattino, il siamese ritornò
miagolando dolcemente
e graffiando alla porta
ancor chiusa.

Sandra gli aprí,
e lui pian pianino
si avvicinò
(con evidente stanchezza)
per farsi prendere in braccio
dalla donna.

Il gatto si fece baciare,

accarezzare,
e, poco dopo,
mangiò un piattone di *purina*
importata dall'America.

Sorridente,
il giovanotto,
si spostò verso la porta.
Non avendo
fatto colazione,
preferì andarsene
al bar in città
per il suo solito caffè,
macchiato.

Alla porta,
ancor sorridente
come un gatto al canarino,
se ne uscí,
assicurandosi volutamente
di chiudere bene la porta
dietro di sè.

Lí, attaccata alla casa
c'è la camera di Sandra Bicce
venuta in Italia
a imparare i costumi
della gente italiana.

MELANCONIA

Leggimi quando sei triste
di melanconia.

Parlo di me e di te,
perchè non c'è ritorno.

Uomo sono come tanti:
il bambino che lascia
e ritorna
al posto natio
ove
tutto è cambiato.

Ecco la tristezza,
il filo interminabile
che non ci lascia mai,
la mia melanconia.

NEBBIA VERONESE

Solo,
guardo gli spiriti viaggiare
nella nebbia furtiva.
Occhi che nel giorno bruciano
dolenti spariscono,
e il cuore batte.

Nell'immensa notte
i pensieri fugaci della passione
si perdono silenziosamente
nell'aria grigia soffocante.

Tutto si muove in un silenzio
misterioso che sembra vita:
baci perduti nei palpiti,
gridi di gioia soffocati.

E tu pazientemente aspetti
udir il suono del treno
che porta l'amore.

Uno strillo rauco
s'infonde nel cuore.

E tu,
                    aspetti?

IL FARO

Bello e pieno di luce,
notte e giorno
risplendi
e mi porti la speranza
quando son solito
perdermi.

Ci saranno venti,
neri come la notte,
ed acque agitate
per naufragarmi.

Come a te è data
la forza per restare,
io
                 vado avanti,
for-se piano,
come una luce offuscata
dall'aurora annuvolata
che d'un tratto prorompe
in strisce
                e stelle
       abbaglianti.

"ALLA LUNA"

Ti vedo, o luna,
sfiorare i monti
e attraversar i queti alberi
i cui rami
tremolano al vento
di una fresca sera,

e penso
ai giorni tristi del poeta
immerso in lacrime.

Perchè egli esce
                  solo
con il tuo sorgere
e si ritira
prima
che a riscaldar vai
un altro cuore,
e perchè
resta sempre rinchiuso
nella tenebra camera
ripensando ai giorni,
passati nel buio,
pur potendo
uscire alla luce?

Avrà avuto paura del sole?

LA LUNA ED IL BAMBINO

Come ti ammiro quando chiara
appari silenziosa nel fondo cielo.
Le stelle luccicano attraverso il velo
della grigia luce che m'è cosí cara.
Mezza luna, luna piena: tutta
ti guardo nelle orbite peregrine,
e non più t'invoco. Miro l'alone
che ti circonda come anima stupefatta.

Ricordo quando bambino, nell'albero,
agitavo i rami; ed io, contento,
aspettavo di veder il vento
spargersi ai pioppi d'oro,
e a te chiedevo invano perchè
con me il vento non tirava.
Sapevo che qualcuno ti originava,
ma chi, dove, e perchè!
T'aspettavo, e dopo, quando tu
silenziosa e chiara t'innalzavi,
io correvo imbizzarrito; tu guardavi
mentre io giocavo pic-a-bu.
Quando tu sfioravi gli alberi
la, limpida, brillavi;
nei miei occhi ti rispecchiavi
lucida e chiara come nei mari
finchè restavo quieto a rimirarti.
Ad un tratto scappavo via via
nascondendomi come una spia
tra solchi di prati profumati.
Che gioia seguire il tuo viso
fra foglie che velavano la tua forma.
Mi muovevo come un bimbo che brama
veder cose cambiar all'improvviso.

Ora non più vado nascondendomi
dietro gli alberi e fra i prati
argentei; non sento più i mirti,
né l'incanto della tua luce avvolgermi.
Adesso aspetto i silenziosi tramonti
che lasciano vermiglie le nuvole
finchè la notte autunnale
li rapisce e crea monti
erranti che il vento dolcemente
sparge attraverso il cielo.

Sembra l'anima, questo velo
che ti copre e discopre lentamente.

Ma ora so che dar inizio al vento
è invano, come tante altre cose
che circondano le nostre case.
Pur contemplo: il volto non è spento.

MALINCONIA DEL NON RITORNO

Sono qua, e penso a te;
leggo il tuo scritto--
una parte minima
un semplice segno
di quello che mi sei stata
uno scritto
privo
del suono della tua voce
il calore della tua anima
l'affetto d'umanità
ridotto
in abbracci--
ora,
            mani tentennanti nel vuoto.

Tutto
come il suono
della nostra voce
che si dilegua in parole
e solo qualche ritmo
incordato all'anima
fa vibrare il cuore
di quel passato
che non c'è più
che non può essere
nemmeno nei segni tuoi scritti
che vogliono preservare
l'intimo di un'anima.

ADAMO

Pomeriggio virgiliano
sulla spiaggia desolata

sabbia calda,
orli fini
di acqua tiepida

una lastra languidamente estesa
ai confini dell'orizzonte
specchiantesi il cielo.

Oasi dello spirito:
contemplazione fuor del pensiero
solamente la vista degli occhi--
trasparente--
in un corpo
di qualche grano di sabbia
sperduto sotto il caldo del sole.

Riflessione senza l'oggetto
luce mistica
come negli occhi illuminati
da fantasmi irregistrabili:

pomeriggio virgiliano--reale,
solo qualche ronzío di mosca
o il languido lambire dell'acqua
su rocce sparse senz'ordine.

Un oggetto nero galleggia
lungo la striscia grigia
d'un braccio di sabbia--
ponte senza inizio
l'approdo sotto i miei piedi
bagnati dall'acqua.
E vedo
da un mare
partorirmi una donna.

CONFESSIONE

Musica,
divinamente
mi arrivi
e investi I miei sensi.

L'anima trema
incontrollabile:

"O Dio!" io dico--
L'estasi esclama!

MOHAWK

Alberi fitti di foglie colorate
riempiono un cielo frettoloso
di ombre gialle e dorate
diffuso in un sereno riposo.

È un mare di foglie in flutto,
di nidi mossi dal vento
dove un crepitío risalta interrotto
nel freddo mohokiano sentiero.

SERA D'OTTOBRE

Penombre di nuvole rosse
affiancano l'orizzonte lontano
sfolgorato di un sole d'autunno
e con se si fonde il mio animo.

La sera silenziosamente scende
nel cinguettío frenetico di uccelli
sugli alberi che non son più di ieri.

NEL CIMITERO MILANESE

Sei meno di un camposanto
di pietre tombali
accatastate in un fianco
presso le ossa
invecchiate
da sette anni;
meno del camposanto
dalla sola fila
di cipressi cuspidali
contenenti il silenzio della morte
impenetrabili
anche al garrulo passero,
alla civetta--
tutto respinto
eccetto il silenzio
che lentamente si prolunga verso il cielo:
sei tu!
cimitero monumentale di Milano
ove gli uccelli cantano
sui rami dell'albero
radicato
presso le ossa
dei sottofondi
nella tomba di Toscanini;
dove
qualche fringuello
aspetta un suo amore,
sopra la statua bronzea
della giovane nuda
come la morte in riposo;
dove mi vedo
nell'immagine di mia figlia
inginocchiata
davanti alla tomba del cugino,

le mani giunte in preghiera
la voce contenuta nell'intimo dell'animo
le labbra mosse
                    ritmicamente;
guardo la donna
quasi invogliare il geranio a voltarsi
e spargere il profumo
sopra
                    la pietra
            del la sua buonanima;

vedo i buoi
sulla terra in discesa
frenati invano
dal povero contadino
sotto l'impietrita immagine
della nostra morte.
I miei occhi
pieni di lacrime
al pianto di mia madre
per il perduto nipote,
il cuore sconvolto
dalle grida di mia sorella
disperata
per la morte del figlio,
la gola che soffoca il mio grido superbo,
"perchè!", perchè,
veramente,
a che vale?

Troppo è la morte per noi:
falso
      il credo
            nel tempo
                  risanatore
delle ferite
          al cuore.

Queste tombe a monumento
non sono da meno
di quelle già accatastate:
son pietre tutte
che s'infrecciano nei cuori,
e solo la morte per via che venga
le discioglie.

Nel tuo cuore
troppe ne saranno state,
mio caro Paolo,
e troppo duro l'involucro del silenzio
più impenetrabile di quello dei cipressi
presso i nostri camposanti.

Quando vedo le lacrime di mia madre
quando sento le grida della tua,
la gola soffoca il mio grido,
e ogni volta,
sento una pietra
entrare nel cuore,
dolorosamente.

Mi rifaccio la strada dei miei cimiteri
ancor più cupo,
più taciturno,
sempre
senza la risposta,

senza la voce che possa,
o no dire
della nostra affinità verso la morte.
Forse,
un giorno,
verrò a trovarti,
quando la capacità di sopportar il dolore
e
la necessità nell'appagarmi in esso
non mi mancheranno.

Nel piazzale davanti al cimitero
l'acciaio del tram mi scuote la mente
come
le grida di tua madre
nel mio cuore.

Un giorno,
forse,
verrò a trovarti.

ASPETTA UN PO'

Se non oggi,
domani
la morte verrà.
Perchè lasciar che venga
se padroni si è di nulla?

Dal momento fecondo,
di nulla si è padroni!

Vivo per soddisfare l'istinto
che, pur,

                    dileguandosi,

con la vecchiaia
cresce in moltiplicità
e più insaziabile.

Chi piange la tua morte?
Tua madre,
tralasciatasi--
tanto dalla stanchezza di lavoro,
sul divano consumato
da gesti continui
e concomitanti
a parole invocatrici
nel perchè
tra gridi e lamenti,
e lacrime
trapassate il fazzoletto
sul cuscino fradicio
da ieri e l'altra sera--
quanto dal continuo dolore
che non va mai via.

Nella sua voce debole
dice:
tutto va bene;
              che vuoi farci;
cosí vuole Dio!

Chi piange la tua morte,
tua madre?
o, chi sa,
se una donna
preservi qualche pensiero
in ricordo
di baci,
o carezze,
non più segnate?

Piange tua madre--
sempre!
Non vuol capire
che se non oggi,
domani
la morte verrà.

Perchè lasciar che venga
non lo capisce,
nè l'accetta:
vane tali spiegazioni
alla madre
che ha fecondato
particelle esigue
in corpi pien di vita.

Vivo per soddisfare
l'istinto dileguante,
aspettando la morte,
forse,
          perchè

        la mia

            ne morrebbe

dal dolore.

Vieni,

ma aspetta un po!

ARRIVA IL GIORNO

Quando sarai morta,
piangerò,
solo.

Nei sogni ti vedrò,
svegliandomi
per il trauma
della tua immagine mancata;
i giorni,
in pensieri ti avrò,
rattristandomi
per il dolore
della tua perduta presenza.

Piangerò,
chi sa quanto;
già le lacrime mi vengono
pensando a quel che dev'essere.

Mi sarai presente
ogn'ora
della mia vita,
ricordandomi
il miracolo della nascita
le carezze ancor qui segnate
il tuo latte
la premurosità,
il tuo bacio di vecchierella
al figlio cresciuto bene;
orgogliosa di Dio
per la maturazione compiuta
della vostra vita.
Piangerò,
come posso non farlo!

POESIA D'AMORE

Finalmente,
la morte mi ha fatto visita:
solamente
un cerchio bianco
immenso e vuoto
resta
nella mente.

Nessun uomo,
nè spirito
a farmi attraversar il fiume,
bagnarmi
di rugiada mattutina,
trasumanar.

Un cerchio vuoto nel sonno,
il ritorno dallo spazio
e il rientro
attraverso
il fuoco geometrico
nel silenzio
d'un tunnel circolare
a non finire.

Fiamme brucianti
impiantantesi
in ogni cellula del pensiero
come stimmate.

Infine, il delirio:
luci prismatiche in circolazione,
immagini pulsanti,
sirene di voci raccapriccianti,
e

il tuo viso!
        ritratto d'angoscia,
                commozione amorosa
per la perdita f atale della vita.

Divina provvidenza! nell'umana
il dolore, il tutto
anche nella morte
in visita.

E quando,
veramente verrà,
tu non ci sarai,
nè Lia da portarmi
alle acque del fiume,
da cui,
        miracolosamente
              scaturisce la vita
                    che ora più amo.

DILUVIO

Picchi di montagne
si alzano al cielo
sparsi
sopra l'acqua
che inonda le case
e le caverne alte
nelle montagne rocciose;
corpi e carcasse galleggiano
intorno agli orli tortuosi,
sorvolati da corvi neri
in gran richiamo;
i piccoli animali,
preda ai grandi,
altrettanto impauriti,
e solo qualche fringuello
saltella,
mentre gli altri uccelli
faticosamente volano
intorno alle vette.

Gli ultimi uomini,
atterriti e in silenzio,
aspettano,
inconsapevolmente,
per ridare all'acqua
                              la vita
che aveva creato.

NUVOLE DALLE VALLI

Silenziosamente
passano le nuvole
tra scogli neri
e lugubri posti.
Pian piano vengono
per i torrenti
montagnosi.

L'albero si soffoca senza parola
e il cielo si arrende
al funebre color.

INVENZIONE

Non c'è nulla
da inventare
su questa terra
perchè c'è tutto.
Dio
ha provveduto.

Tutto è scoperta,
da quando l'occhio s'apre
al momento che si chiude

ed uno vede
più o meno come vuole
più che come può.

APRILE

Vivere?
Rivivere!
Il ramo
infiora
o
cade
alla terra:

un attimo,
un sempre.

Rivivere?
Vivere!

IL GIRASOLE

Nasci per prendere
il sole.

All'alba
gli alzi la testa
per riceverlo.

Quando scende
l'orizzonte,
abbassi la testa
sul tuo collo contorto

Con ogni semi-giro
riaizi la testa
sempre più grande
sul collo strozzato.

Quando, infine,
t'inchini alla terra,
veniamo a stringerti
l'olio solare.

Noi,
stramazzati la testa,
che ne sarà!

Perchè!
Per chí?

CRISTO EBREO

Chi sei tu, Michele?

Un nome
la cui persona risponde
all'ordine, oggi
della falce e martello,
della camicia rossa
come ieri della nera, domani
chi sa,
anche del cordone francescano
in fervida estasi,
finanche con i piedi nudi
sul carbone rosso?

Facciamo di Cristo un ebreo
sebbene sia figlio di Dio,
uomo prima, e, divino,
e non ebreo o dio.

Michele,
          dove sei?
                    Michele!

CONCLUSI

Non voglio fare
la vita dei conclusi,
né vegetare
pur nell'attività.

Non voglio attenermi
alla filosofia
che m'imprigioni,
al partito
che faccia di me
un mezzo.

Questi,
                    tutti,
hanno il fine
di assoggettarmi,
farmi seguace:

mantenere
la nostra voce, bianca,
castrandoci.

DOPO LA MORTE

Alla morte
vorrei credermi
frutta matura
coltivata,
il grano
trebbiato da pane,
la lupinella,
il vitello
a sfamare
le bocche dal pianto,
il passero all'aquila,
gli insetti medesimi!

Credermi
anima
pur nell'infinito.

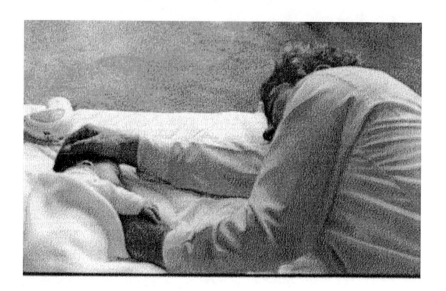

TROMBA

Alfieri m'apparve in una visione
che non era sogno,
visione
di raggi di luce abbagliante.

La tromba, grave,
spargeva il suo pianto
per tutto un camposanto
popolato
da vivi più che da morti.

Nessuno ti sente
non un uomo ascolta il tuo suono.
Il tarlo
ha penetrate ogni cellula,
e ora comanda;
ci ha cambiato tanto
che oggi siam rossi
come ieri neri,
e noi stessi,
        mai!

VITTORIO ALFIERI

Quelle nevi
agghiacciate dal sangue
di madri italiane
ancor in attesa,
e quelle ivi, forse
dovutamente rassegnate,
non portan alcun segno.

La tua voce
è il fischio
sentito dal cane!

Other books by ADOLPH CASO

AMERICA'S ITALIAN FOUNDING FATHERS by Adolph Caso includes works by Beccaria and Mazzei. Cloth, ill., ISBN 0-8283-1640-4, $25.95

DANTE IN THE 20TH CENTURY by Adolph Caso et al includes articles by several American and European scholars on Dante. Ill., ISBN 0-9378-3216-2, $25.95.

ISSUES IN BILINGUAL AND FOREIGN LANGUAGE EDUCATION by Adolph Caso recounts the plight of limited English-speaking students and their struggle to introduce Italian language into our public schools. ISBN 0-8283-2066-7, $14.95.

LIVES OF ITALIAN AMERICANS--They Too Made This Country Great by Adolph Caso has 50 biographies of those who contributed in the formation of the U.S. Cloth, ill., ISBN 0-8283-1699-6, $15.95.

MASS MEDIA VS. THE ITALIAN AMERICANS by Adolph Caso explores, critically, the image and ethnic profiling of Italian Americans. Paper, ill., ISBN 0-8283-1831-X, $4.95.

ODE TO AMERICA'S INDEPENDENCE by Vittorio Alfieri is the first such composition written on the emerging na-tion, in Italian and translated into English by Adolph Caso. Paper, ISBN 0-8283-1667-8, $11.95.

ON CRIMES AND PUNISHMENTS by Cesare Beccaria influenced Jefferson, Adams, Washington and many more. To a great degree, America owes its present form of government on this book. This book is widely used in university and college classes throughout the U.S. Introduction and commentary by Adolph Caso. Paper, ISBN 0-8283-1800-X, $5.95.

ROMEO AND JULIET--Original Text of Masuccio, Da Porto, Bandello, and Shakespeare. Edited and with an Introduction by Adolph Caso. "A rose by any other name would smell as sweet." Cloth, ISBN 0-937832-4, $19.95.

STRAW OBELISK The by Adolph Caso deals with the effects of World War II on a southern Italian village. Cloth, Ill. 0-8283-2005-5, $24.95.

TO AMERICA AND AROUND THE WORLD--The Logs of Columbus and Magellan by Christopher Columbus and Antonio Pigafetta contains the first reports on the first voyage to America and the first voyage around the world, edited and with an introduction and commentary by Adolph Caso. Paper, ISBN 0-8283-2063-2, $18.95.

TUSKEGEE AIRMEN-- *The Men Who Changed A Nation.* Charles E. Francis. 4th Edition--Revised, UpDated and Enlarged by Colonel Adolph Caso. Long before the Civil Rights move-ment, the Tuskegee Airmen were already living and fighting for equality. As a result, by integrating the Armed Forces, they integrated the whole nation. Their combat feats in Italy have become legendary. This volume of 500 pages contains photos, appendix and an Index of 25 pages. ISBN 0-8283-2077-2, Paper, $24.95.

WATER AND LIFE by Adolph Caso contains photos and poems in the original English and Italian. Paper, illustrated, ISBN 0-8283-2079-9, $14.95.

WE, THE PEOPLE--Formative Documents of America's Democracy by Adolph Caso contains original documents and lengthy commentary on the formation of America's Demo-cracy: *Mayflower Compact, On Crimes and Punishments, Declara-tion of Causes, Declaration of Independence, Articles of Confedera-tion, Constitution, Bill of Rights, Amendments, Emanci-pation Proclamation, Promissory Note,* Cloth, Ill. ISBN 0-8283-2006-3, $22.95.

YOUNG ROCKY--A True Story of Attilio (Rocky) Cas-tellani by Kinney-Caso tells the life story of a great boxer. Paper, ill., ISBN 0-8283-1802-2, $11.95.